Seeds
are for
Sharing

Seeds *are for* Sharing

RECLAIMING SPIRIT

Poems by
Dawn Smoke

Illustrations by Jackie Traverse

Medicine Wheel Publishing

This book touches on topics of addiction, intergenerational trauma, and other triggering subjects. If you need to speak with someone, please contact the Hope for Wellness Helpline 24/7 by phone at 1-855-242-3310 (toll-free) or by chat at www.hopeforwellness.ca.

Medicine Wheel Publishing acknowledges that we live and work on the traditional and unceded lands of the Coast Salish People, including the T'Sou-ke People, the W̱SÁNEĆ People, Sc'ianew People, and the lək̓ʷəŋən Peoples.

Cover Design by Jeff Werner
Cover Art © Jackie Traverse
Family Photos provided by Dawn Smoke, Silvaine Zimmermann
Edited by Lisa Frenette

ISBN 9781778540592

Published 2025 by Medicine Wheel Publishing in Canada.
www.medicinewheelpublishing.com

Printed in PRC

10 9 8 7 6 5 4 3 2 1

Funded by the Government of Canada | Financé par le gouvernement du Canada | Canada

Contents

I'd like to dedicate this book to the thousands of my People
who went through RESIDENTIAL SCHOOLS and suffered
at the behest of the corporate colonial canadians
and their genocidal and murderous programs against my Peoples.

I'd like to dedicate it to the thousands of Children
who lost their lives in their institutions.

I'd like to dedicate it to the thousands of Children
who were damaged similarly in the DAY SCHOOLS.

And I'd like to dedicate it to the sixties scooped Children,
Families and Communities that suffered
through loss of language, spirit, culture.
May those memories remain with us always, may the spirits
of our ancestors guide us into a new light and day.

Aho.

Prologue

THERE WAS A TIME WHEN THE WORLD SPUN ON ITS OWN, without questioning its existence. The world existed in a silent void, waiting for the whisper of the universe to awaken it, the breath of Creator to set its soul on fire...for life to form and micro-organisms to spew forth from the seabed.

The hydro-thermal vents existed 4.28 billion years ago. Our creation stories began shortly after this...for in universal time the difference of millions from billions differs little, like the formation of the first sponge to the Spirit of the muskrat or the turtle...The world had begun to spin, the earth to breathe. Our stories began to form. The language of life had begun, and this story I am sharing now had its beginnings.

Always there is a beginning and it's always at the start.

We begin with two young Anishinaabe girls. Neither could walk or talk as of yet. They were new beings on Mother Earth. Their words hadn't formed yet. Their limbs could not carry them. Their Spirits were coming to terms with new life forms, their eyes open and dim, shapes forming, bodies disconnected from the warmth of the liquid amniotic fluid connection that comforted them.

There was a loneliness that seemed strange and alien. A distance from the bond that only you and your family possessed, from that female presence that was with you and comforted you. You both missed something, but you weren't sure what it was.

You and your Sister shared a real warm feeling. Was that it? That body that wasn't there anymore? That was the answer to the missing part of you. The disappearance of fundamental need. Something indescribable, each of you turning to the other in the murkiness of your new being. At last you had solace in each other. You had your Sister. You had Susie.

The dimness slowly receded, the vision becoming clearer. The exchange of a grimace turned into a smile of recognition. You had each other...You both were one, snuggling, comforting each other. Fingers intertwined, eyes beginning to see, the clarity, the strength, becoming reality. The sound of beating hearts, the feel of eyelids fluttering, the gurgling of your other half, still yearning for that something missing.

This place you were in, this white, empty-sounding and looking and feeling place, was cold. You both felt the coldness and you reached for each other to share warmth, but no one else was there to hold onto, no one to utter words or pick you up. You now knew fear.

The strangers briefly glanced over at us, sending shivers through our bodies. We couldn't speak yet; our brains were forming and taking time to mature. I just looked at my Sister and shared a mutual fear. The dread of being defenceless.

No one seemed to like either of us, whether for foster or adoption. These words came out of their mouths often. In the meantime, we were put in a room with other little ones and bigger ones, all crying and sad. Some made words, crying "Mommy." Was that what was missing, something called mommy?

Time goes on. I could understand more. Eyes and legs and hands and brain were growing up, living in that empty place with other kids, sad and crying constantly. It was hard not to be sad. At least we had each other, my Sister and I. We understood the word love now, even though no one said it or showed it. We knew it because we loved each other.

One day a nurse came in and bathed us, dressed us, and was chatting away—something about fostering us. We were petrified. Strangers came in...lots of talk between the grown-ups, lots of smiles. The strangers picked us up and walked outside. We never remembered ever being outside. The feel, the smells. No idea what was happening. These grown-ups never spoke to us. When we cried, we never expected much except to be ignored or smacked and told to shut up. These grown-ups were no different. We were still ignored. We were taken to another building, put in another room, the door was closed, and we waited and waited.

No one came. We were hungry. Our diapers needed changing.

Night came. No one came. We were so scared, so hungry.

My Sister reached out her hands. *Hold me*, she said.

Finally, my diaper was being changed. A loud slap. The poop was wiped in my face. I cried. My Sister cried. Watery milk was our sustenance. Silence our companion. One day, one of the adults we used to see come into the room, picked us up to take us to the doctor for a checkup. Both of us were underweight from our starvation diet. My bum was red with rash and my legs had welts. We never went back to that second place. We went to our first place, where we felt safe for a short time. We had attention from the nurse who bathed us and changed us.

Off we went again, Susie and I, only this time I was frantic.

They put my Sister in another car.

We screamed.

Dawn and her daughter, Charlie

a Glimpse, a Seed, an Offering...

THIS WRITING IS JUST A BIT OF ME WRITTEN DOWN, with much left out, giving a glimpse into a life...

So many of those memories had been hidden from me for so long...

A life of drama, of laughter, of much that had to be overcome, of adventure and dreams and growth, of moments remembered...

This is just an old woman, an old Indigenous woman, trying to share parts of her life, an Anishinaabe Kwe who had a few things to mull over and speak about. And possibly, this exercise here may allow the floodgates of memory to open and maybe there will be some young brown-skinned woman who'll say to herself, "Oh, I can relate; I've been there too. I'm not alone." Maybe she'll find comfort in my jottings...

This is sort of an autobiography, but not a full one. Too many holes, black spots. It is a story of some of the moments in my life that you might find interesting.

If not, well, that just means you weren't with me, or have little imagination, or just can't relate. Lol, makes no nevermind to me, won't stop me from talking, though I have to admit, if it wasn't for my Daughter, Charlie Smoke, I never would have bothered.

She kept nudging me to the point of annoyance...then months went by and it was just, *why not?*

I have left quite a bit out, from either lack of memory, or just not wanting to share, or protecting those involved, or just big, black patches where there's no recall, or wanting to forget...

I get glimpses I'm not thrilled with and so just block them out...

My business anyhow and no one else's. No need for therapy, since I long ago handled it all. My therapy has been to bury things and then just move on.

Perhaps not the healthiest way, but it works for me.

I'm not a fount of wisdom, but I have lived a life, a full one, had my share of adventures and struggles. I've lived through a lot of loving times, also a lot of painful times, lots of pleasures of all types, and like so many others, lots of tears and depression and hard agonies.

I've had my moments but never thought they were really that unique, I guess, but that's only because I never gave it much thought. That's why I didn't think my life was interesting enough to put to paper, till those around me convinced me that there was enough living done and unique moments lived that, yes, others might find my lifetime interesting...

I learned and opened myself up as much as possible to the possibilities in this life. I've managed to travel much of our lands, all four directions. I was given the name Sees In Four Directions by the Seminole. I also carry, and am honoured to carry, two other names given in ceremony. I've met and spent time with many of our Native Nations. I grew from darkness and constant struggle to where I feel I live a life blessed and have come to a place of light and comfort. A place that the Cree have a word for: Kiyam, pronounced key yam.

I was told it is a place of balance, a place where you are at comfort and at peace; pretty well anything negative is rejected. That doesn't mean you live in a Mary Poppins world, or you're sitting meditating with the Buddha; it means you don't allow the blackness to creep in anymore and nest. Hope is always kept alive and all is balanced...

In this hard-fought place, I have absolutely no depression, though I admit there is a deep-set sadness with humanity in general. No thoughts of suicide anymore, just a heart of gratitude. No longer struggling with love, or money, or my shortcomings, or the meanness of humanity, or my dark shadows, or emptiness, or just plain soul pain. Of course, this also has to do with my age. Wisdom of some sort can come with age and living, not always, but sometimes. And it doesn't mean my heart is immune to the pathetic blackness we face in this day and age. The shadows are there; the trick is to give them no power.

I'm also no longer struggling with my overwhelming anger and fury, or lack of trust, or the frustration of other people's shortcomings. It all exists around me still, but I refuse to allow it any control, and can verbalise loudly and easily and vent with the best. I have developed what I think is a good sense of humour, even though it's hell quite often, sitting listening to jokers. But, thankfully, I just put it all down to their own lack, never mine, lol! I've armed myself with patience and compassion when I survey my world. Have gathered over time a wide circle of Friends and Extended Family and Cousins and adopted Children and discovered blood Family, and I cherish them all.

From a kid who had no friends in her world, to a Woman who is surrounded with strands of Jewels and Love all over Her country.

Creator takes care of me, never more than I need, but always exactly what I need at the moment. I need little and that's one of the keys, I think, that helped me to this place I'm in. My wants and needs are pretty simple. I really have little ego, but walk the world proudly, knowing I'm doing o.k., that I am o.k., that I've survived my monsters...

I have no tolerance for greed, ownership, lust for money, racism, egotists, sexism, cruelty to anyone or anything, genderism, ageism, or just plain evil, where others wantonly cause pain, cause heartache, cause death.

I have absolutely no tolerance for those unthinking humans who put their needs above all things and are destroying my Planet, my Mother Earth. I personalise this in the first person, hoping at some point we will all do the same. Every living thing on this Planet is my Family. I have a responsibility towards Her health and happiness. I am part of everything, and everything is part of me. The Land, The Waters, The Air, every Creature big and small, every blade of Grass and Tree and Flower...every Rock and Grain of Sand...

We all are one; without each other we die.

We are Stardust and for what reason we've been put here, I have no idea. What I do know, for my own reality, is that we all have purpose, therefore there is a Creator and a Magic in our universe. There are Magic happenings all around us, or as some like to call magic, "miracles," that we can observe daily.

The fact we wake up each day, breathe, hear the birds singing while we drink our coffee, or say our prayers, or do our exercises, is magic. Thus, our prayers of thanksgiving and gratitude each morning strengthen us and the world around us.

We all are one;
without each other we die.

Love is all encompassing.
As is Integrity and Honour.
A willingness to step forward and step between to protect.
To nourish those around you,
both in the physical and spiritual.
To not judge those who are just trying to survive.
To be a part of your Community, Family, Circle and World.
Knowing every living entity has its place.
We are all dependent on one another.
The Bear is Our Brother.
The Earth Our Mother.
Water is Life.
We are all connected.

The Residential Schools
set up to destroy "the Indian,"
by kidnapping us Kids from Our Communities
and sending us to schools,
sometimes thousands of miles away,
where it was normal to be abused,
have our hair cut,
starved,
sexually abused,
beaten,
forced to forget we were "Indian."
Where Culture, Language, Family and Name were taken away.
Some spent these years in those schools "just fine."
Overwhelming numbers, though, suffered through hell.
Some were used in medical experiments,
some never made it back Home,
dead from trying to get Home or
dead from abuse by nuns and priests...
"The Indian Problem" would finally be rectified,
or so the powers that be thought.
Kill "the Indian" and the exploitation of Our Lands
and Resources would open up;
the canadian government and banks and
corporations could have free rein
and their coffers would fill...

The call of blood is strong.
The more Native they looked,
the more racism they faced in the outside world
that always said "they were different."
Loneliness, always a lot of loneliness.
Small children, not understanding, nothing ever explained,
just feeling empty, lonely and sad.
This program took away Our Language.
Took Our Names,
Our Families,
Our Community,
Our Culture,
Our History,
Our Stories,
Our way of Being.

—

The genocide has been going on since colonialism first began.
Our Women and Children were always targeted first.
The Women had their power removed,
the Women's Clans banned,
the territories' traditional leadership disregarded
and replaced with a colonial construct.
christian church and government working hand in hand...
Our Ceremonies and Celebrations banned,
Our Spiritual Items stolen,
Our Bones dug up and put on display.
Even Our People taken and displayed in Zoos.
Our Women's place in Our Community
warped into a white man's perception.
No more Clan Mothers,
No more Women's Lodges...
Then they took their choice of Women...
Then they took the Children...
They kept controls on Our Men who had their dignity removed,
Hunting and games and Ceremony restricted or banned,
Taught that Our Women were not to be
held in good standing anymore,
Taught that they, the Men, were worth nothing,
and the Women less,
no longer Warriors,
Protectors,
no longer Hunters,
Providers...
They were taught
that their People were nothing but savages,
pathetic, idiotic, uneducated, stupid, lazy, alcoholic savages
needing to be taken care of and babysat
by the crown
and by government

and the christian churches…

The christian churches that were the tools of colonialism,
the sword that was used to help in our destruction...
The main weapon used in our genocide...
Working hand in hand with the governments of the day...
Manipulating us with their gods and prophets...
Mind-fucking us with their religions...
The only way at the end was trading Our Spirituality
for a religion drenched in blood.
Most of us did pray to their gods
in order to survive...
Those were the days
of Our Fathers and Grandfathers...
of Our Mothers and Grandmothers...
of Our Aunties and Uncles…
But We, in the present,
We survived...
Time has moved on...
We're in the act of reclamation...
The ways of Our Great-Greats...
The ways of Our Ancestors...
The ways of our Original Peoples...
We reclaim Our Spirituality
and Our Spirits...
We have survived and are rebounding
and regaining our strength and unity and beauty...
We are One Nation of many Nations
on this continent of Turtle Island
and
We are Resilient.

Many Nations are gone,
except for their sighs still resonating in the woods
...the cries of the Babies
...the lamenting of the Women.
Many were lost in the fogs of history.
Only memories remain,
kept alive by other Indigenous Nations' stories,
or the odd footnote in the white man's history books,
or perhaps a street name in some small town...
Gone.
Except for the voices of the Spirits that can still be heard,
and the knowledge of where we might walk now.
All is covered with the blood of the murdered;
the air still full of the cries of their death songs.
Our continent was not "won" in a war of honour.
It was won by murder and lies and subterfuge,
by the horrific decimation of our many Nations,
by the illnesses brought over.
It was won by greed;
it was won by murderous intent.
We watched as Our Land was claimed
by those without love for Her.
This Land cries with the hundreds of thousands, possibly millions,
brought down by illnesses,
and a hundred thousand other deadly horrid ways of dying.
Our bodies could not fight against an enemy we'd never seen,
nor experienced.
Biological warfare.
Outright killing.
Bounties.
Whole Villages, whole Peoples wiped out violently.
Starvation.
Theft.

We People now take pride and comfort in the fact that we survived,
and continue to grow in strength and numbers.
But many are broken.
A small number are not even aware of their blood and history.
Total assimilation.
Brainwashed.
Traumatized.
There are those children who are lost to themselves and their People.
Lost in a haze of drugs and liquid poisons.
Just here, not alive, not dead, trying to feel nothing.
Dead inside or working their way there.
Loss of Hope…potential suicide...
Suicide.
There are those "light-skinned" ones,
content to fit into the white man's world and "pass."
Those who pose as Native
and accept the white man's "largesse" for themselves.
Those sacrificing their own People in the
quest for money and power.
Those twisted between two cultures,
trying to blend christianity with the traditional beliefs of Our Peoples.
Many, many are assimilated.
Many lost to themselves, their families, their communities,
waiting to be found and offered hope.
They are called lost birds,
waiting for a hand to be stretched out,
waiting for their People to call their name,
waiting to hear their name called once more
and for the Spirits to recognize that name
and for their People to reach out and pull them in...

Many are finding their way back on their own,
to a place where Our Ancestors would be proud.
Many of Our People are Blessed and
Strong and Wise and Caring.
Those whom Creator put here in our midst as
Helpers, Healers and History Keepers,
Story Tellers,
Protectors of their People and the Land,
of the Earth and Air
and all that inhabit Our Mother.
Those who constantly remind us:
We are One with all Creator's gifts.
One with all Life.
One with Mother Earth.
We are Mother Earth,
all living Spirits.
We are all part of Mother Earth.

THE LANGUAGE I'M USING is the language given me by the colonials, after they took mine and left me where I can't reclaim my own tongue. This is partly due to a bit of a brain malfunction; I've never had a good memory and focus is a bit off, has been since young—though I abused alcohol and drugs, it started way before my own struggles. Nothing too serious, because when it's really needed, I'm on point 100%. This brain thing unfortunately was brought on by years of self-abuse and physical trauma (and from "not just a bit of" genocidal policy) that had left my Birth Mother an alcoholic, sick and broken and angry, for most of Her life.

I was born in 1949 at Toronto General Hospital; that's in Ontario, Canada. Children's Aid was in my life soon after, moments, actually. Mom and her Sisters all had moved to Toronto from Lindsey, after my Grandmother Margaret had crossed over, followed by my Grandfather a year later—there was nothing left to keep them in Lindsey. My Great-grandfather was Chief Joseph Whetung, the father of my Grandmother Margaret Whetung, of Curve Lake, who was the wife of my Grandfather Albert Smoke.

Mom and her Sisters got pregnant, alcohol dependent, and their Children were removed, so the story went. Not because of her being an alcoholic, but it's what the government and Children's Aid were doing in those days, scooping Us, stealing Us. No Father was listed in my case, but since then, I learned that many Fathers' names were not recorded. None of the Smoke Family were approached to take us in; many Smokes were being scooped.

Mom was a street-toughened Woman with a reputation that "no one messes with Her or Her Sisters." She survived any way she could and protected her Sisters to the best of her abilities. Funny thing that I should mention is that they all lived in the same area of Toronto that Frank, my older Brother, used to hang out in. He made contact with our Mom and Aunties. Not a good one, since Frank and Mom and the Sisters were all dysfunctional. Now, this was also where I was working as a Counsellor and Life Skills Coach just a couple of years after Frank left the streets. We were only three years different in age, so our paths must have even crossed back then. Who knows? I didn't know Frank yet, that would be long into the future, and I never knew my Birth Mom or Aunties, though we must have crossed paths.

Frank told me about my Mom. It seems Winnie Smoke, Frank and I knew some of the same folk, but no one told me there might be a family connection, just a block or so away. I think they were protecting me...Millie Redmond of Council Fire knew Winnie well, knew me well (appreciate it, Millie, I got to know her in a different way than the sadness she was in then).

Some of those maladies, physical and mental and spiritual, were passed onto us Children. Once, when I worked at a Women's drop-in, I walked into the living room when one old lady smiled and said, "Hi Maggie."

Her friend said clearly, "You meant 'Winnie' and that's Dawn." She said her friend couldn't remember much of anything anymore and just got me confused with an old friend they hadn't seen in years...

Yup, now I know, it was probably my Mom that she was referring to. They said I looked just like her...Looking at a picture years later, I saw no resemblance. I should share, though, that when I finally saw her face in that photo, it was one of those "moments" where the world shook...

The very first time I had Her actual Face; some of you may know what I'm meaning.

One of those sixties scoop moments.

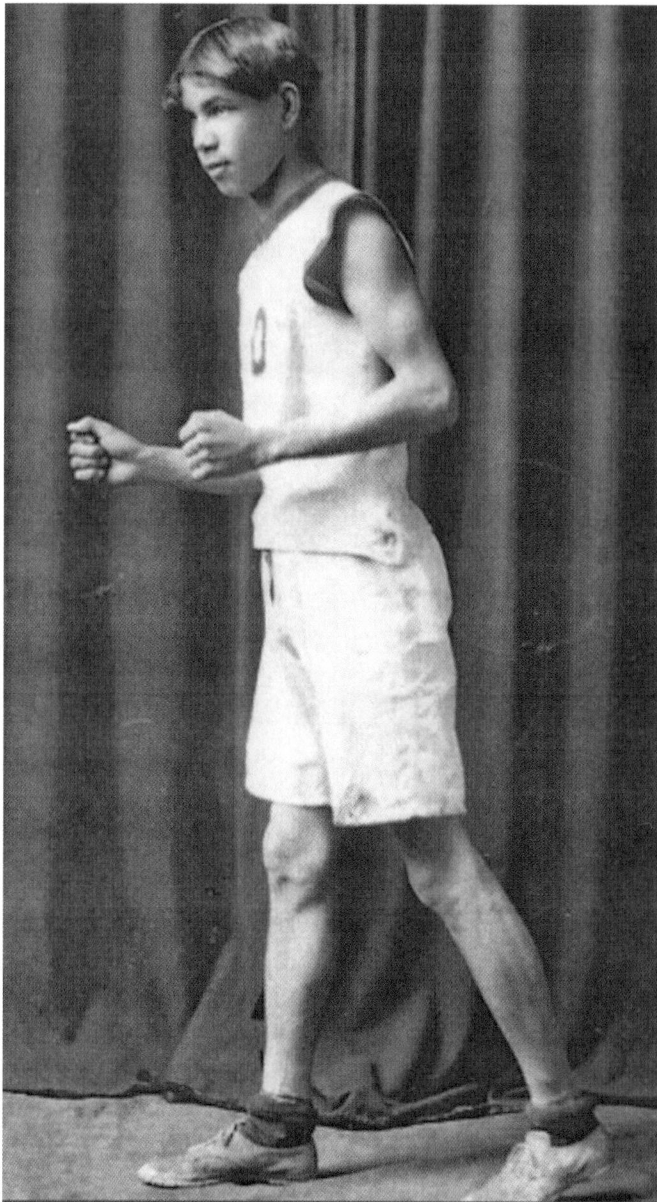

Grandfather Albert Smoke (1922 Olympics)

Great-grandfather Chief Joseph Whetung

Winnie Smoke and her siblings

Winnie Smoke

sixties scoop
To have everything taken away
from you as soon as you're born.
To have no one to love or to hold
you or in many cases protect you.
To be abused without anyone
hearing or seeing or caring.
To have your trust destroyed.
To cry alone in the dark at an age
where you have no idea why you
feel so sad or scared,
why your loneliness and aching
overshadowed everything.

A bit of a Biographical piece, limited from a lack of knowledge
and memories gone…but those remembered are vivid:
When the social worker, Mrs. Cassiar, walked with me hand
in hand, on my way to my adoptive parents' house,
I remember the feelings I had;
I remember saying I didn't want to go.
I remember my doll, Susie.
I remember it being coolish and I had on a coat and hat;
I remember being scared and angry—very, very angry.
My emotions locked behind a deadpan look.
A knock on the door.
The new Mother looking in the round hallway mirror,
fluffing her hair, while the new Father opened the door.
I was three.

Young Dawn

LOOKING BACK NOW, I can feel just how excited they must have been. Really wasn't their fault I just wanted out of there. An abused 3-year-old who cried her heart out at Christmas, because of all the presents under the tree; trying to understand that these "gifts" were a normal thing that time of year and they were for me.

I remember that first day sitting in a highchair while they tried to get me to talk to them and eat ice cream. I remember how upset they were when I kept saying no. They really were trying to get me to love them; it took time, but slowly I started trusting them a bit.

One day, asking the adoptive Mom if she really was going to be my real Mom. If she was going to keep me forever. I'd been fostered out a few times before I was three—not putting this down to garner anyone's sympathy, but to illustrate that Children feel, they are very sensitive. Unless they become "dead" inside. Their sensitivity dies, the capability to love dies if it's not shown in their early years. Many adopted kids may have been through a lot, and their stories get buried inside them. It takes a good amount of love and compassion to make them feel "safe," to get them to "trust." Unfortunately, many adoptive parents lack the training needed and most foster parents have no skills.

In 1952, foster parents made $1.48 a day—decent money. A loaf of bread ran about 15 cents. Now, hopefully, this has changed somewhat, but back then, I think it was just assumed that, if you were white and christian, you must be good with kids. One of my cousins had a pot of hot tea poured over him by a foster mother. In his 80's now, the scars are still there on his chest and Spirit. Children's Aid never really did that much filtering when it came to foster homes, so many Children were permanently scarred in foster situations that were nothing but abusive. This happened for so many Indigenous Children when the government and its lackeys decided to steal us Kids any way they could and attempt our assimilation.

Reading my report from Children's Aid, they had every reason to assume I'd have no problem being adopted because I was "quiet and good-looking"...their actual words! My poor Brother Frank hadn't a chance of being adopted with a wasted arm and scrunched-up eye... That's it, "quiet and good-looking" got you the so-called "magic ticket" to adoption where you'd at least get to stay in one place, good or bad... The rest, who didn't fit the bill, were fostered.

House to house, experience to experience, for years.

If they were lucky, someone may hold them and say something positive. Maybe show them some affection. We were kept apart, stolen, from Our Families and Communities, from Our Language, Our Histories, Our Culture, even Our Names were taken...

We were supposed to turn into wee white kids and, eventually, good canadian, church-going citizens...

We've lost so many through suicide and drugs and alcohol, and mental breakdowns and depressions and the jails, and many came from this system of child theft. Genocide through assimilation. War against Children, all of it.

The 60's scoop lawsuit goes from 1951 and up, but I've talked to those older than me who remembered the same thing happening in the 30's and 40's. Then of course, there were the residential schools, and the day schools.

I had my Brother for ten years, till he crossed over—eaten away by cancer. Lovely man by the time we connected, but it took him a lifetime of healing from wounds all related to the 60's scoop to become the good man he truly was—the story of most of us 60's scoopers who carried our soul pain through hell and made it out the other side. Anyhow, a good man who tried to help as many people who were rock bottom as he could. He had boundless love for and from so many...Creator blessed us both by bringing us together just in time to enjoy our sibling-hood, and for me to help him in his last couple of years...

During all of this, I also found our younger Brother Dan, who lives in Ontario in a care home, a sweet, gentle bear of a man...So now I have my Mohawk Sister Deb and my younger Ojibway Brother Dan...

Hope I still have time to find my other Sisters. I heard one may have been scooped to Europe...I may have one out on the eastern islands, not sure, possibly Nova Scotia.

I'm just sitting here with you and talking...an old lady, sitting, talking, rambling on, musing, the only sounds are the fire crackling and the music of the lake just right over there...I'm hoping there may be a few words in all this that may touch you in some way...that can reassure you in your own struggles. I do want to make sure that you know, deep inside, that you are not alone, we never are. All many of us can really aspire to, I think, is touching one another in a positive way, without expectations, without judgements.

There are many personal opinions here, I profess no truths, just opinions and what I've personally observed or lived. My own take on everything: "no one owns the truth." My words are only something to ponder on, or perhaps ignore; we all live our own lives and experience and observe things differently...

My memories are mine alone, as are my words. Truth is always Truth and History remains as it is.

There are stories in Curve Lake of big black cars
coming and scooping whatever kids were standing around.
Stories of the Women, when they saw these big black cars coming,
they would grab as many kids as they could
and hustle all off to the bush.
No paperwork or permission, just kids taken, "disappeared."
Remembering too that many of the adults were
RESIDENTIAL SCHOOL kids at one time,
or had Children in RESIDENTIAL SCHOOL.
The fear would be palpable.

I WAS FOSTERED 3 TIMES by the time of my adoption at three. I was damaged physically, mentally, spiritually, and most of all, emotionally. My Brother Frank was fostered out—I've no idea how many times.

He went from unhappy situation to miserable situation over and over, being beaten...never having a sense of being loved or belonging, trying to survive...filled with rage, filled with hate, spending so many years of his life incarcerated.

He found his way and got to spend his later years learning about his people, reaching out, helping street folk and the elderly. He made a special place on this planet for many damaged souls. A very Good Man, despite all he'd been through. I had the Honour to travel with Frank and my Daughter Charlie to Ontario, connecting with Our Cousins and visiting Our Territory.

Frank had only been there when young and rough. He had doubts, worried his Relations may not accept him. He'd connected to some of them, years ago, when he was still a street criminal (a very bad street criminal, who was almost always caught). We tried to get him to understand that he was no longer the rough man they'd known, that he was a different Man now, and it was time to allow them to love him. And they did. It was wonderful to see his smile.

We shared a wonderful fish fry that our Cousins hosted at Curve Lake. Frank hadn't ever met many of Our Family, hadn't met some for years. He was proud to finally meet his Family; proud to do it after he became the Man he had become. He had bonded with his Cousins Ben and Maria a few years before this, and we both had the pleasure of sharing their company for a few days. Cousin Maria had worked on a

SMOKE family tree. They'd signed onto ancestry.com and could connect us to a few more Cousins.

At the fish fry, Frank told me quietly that this was the very first time he had felt Family Love, and that it was the best trip he'd ever had. We knew he wouldn't have long left to spend with us. Cancer was already attacking him. It meant so much to him to spend time with his Niece, my Daughter Charlie. Wonderful to see the bond they had. In our last days together, I gave him his medicine bundle. Charlie came and sang for her Uncle...He had his medicine song/death song.

Then I got the Honour of leading him over. It helped him to cope with the pain and helped him to let go of this world. I told him:

Look Frankie! See all Our Ancestors, Our Relations,
holding out their hands for you to come with them,
it's time...
There's Our Mom, Frank, looking so good, all healed and
healthy and beaming eyes and filled with Love and
Welcoming you,
All of Our Beautiful Relations, radiating love and light
and they've made the biggest fish fry just for you, Brother,
Honouring your Wonderful Self into the Circle...
Grandma and Grandpa are smiling to see their Grandson
and finally getting to hug you
Your Cousins, Your Uncles,
All Our Old Ones, Frank!

On and on, I talked to Brother. Went out for a tea, and coming back in, there was Frank, in his bed, waving and pointing at the corner of his room, smiling. He was seeing them...He left that night.

I know he's good. I thank Creator for bringing us together when it was needed. Both older and wiser, and neither of us were fragmented in our loneliness. I still have my Mohawk Sister Deb, my Father's Daughter. She was also adopted out. We spent some years together, before I left Ontario. Loved her then and love her now, so happy there was a reconnection.

I also have my other younger Anishinaabe Brother, Dan. We are getting to know each other, now that Frank has left. Lovely, Huge Gentle Bear of a Man, in a care home, being taken care of well, and also helping out there. He's the youngest of Winnie's kids. Frank and I went to meet him in Ontario, in the fall of 2018. Left the boys to bond.

Now Frank's gone, it's my turn.

Older brother Frank

Younger brother Dan

Sister Deb

Dan and Frank meeting

MY ADOPTIVE FATHER was a full-blood but assimilated Mohawk, who tried his best to be invisible. He married an Irish woman. They adopted me and they adopted my Mohawk Sister Deb. Our Mohawk Relations—those that I knew in my early beginnings—became invisible. They seldom darkened the doors. I was told years later, by an Auntie, that it was because they were made to feel uncomfortable by the Mother. Perhaps so. I asked the Mother one time, when young, why they didn't visit; why I hardly got to see them after my Grandmother "died." She never did answer me. She seemed angry.

When I was first adopted, I was miserable and wanted nothing to do with anyone. Asocial I guess...damaged. Three foster homes by three-years-old, unhealthy, rickets, skin and bones, till I was "adopted," and they fattened me up, or so my adoptive Mother told me. My adoptive Mother had to go to work and I was babysat by my Father's Mom, my Grandma Emma Elmes (Beauvais). She told me that one thing I should always remember is that "I'm a good Mohawk girl and I was worth the world." And not to pick my nose in public!

Once, when we were out walking, we passed a fella...nose picking; I pointed it out. Ha! Grandma was angry; she went on and on about it all day!

I loved that Woman. She was the first Person whom I loved, ever. Her and my doll Susie that came with me before I was adopted (no idea who gave me Susie, but she comforted me and gave me someone to talk to and keep all my secrets). My new Mother took her to the doll hospital often, to fix her face and hands, from me sucking on her constantly. Susie, my best friend. I think Susie connected me to someone who had shown me some affection at some point.

Grandmother crossed over when I was almost 5; I only had her a year or two. It was night-time, I was sitting on the top of the stairs, listening to the adults talking. I was devastated. Didn't understand anything about "death," but did understand that Grandma had left me and I was alone again. Didn't understand why my Father was sobbing.

As a little girl, I walked into Grandma's house. There in the hallway was a head statue of an Iroquois (Haudenosaunee) Warrior. The hallway was dark. The warrior had eyes that shone in the dark, war paint and fury on his face, and a tomahawk in his upraised arm. Above this on the wall hung some artwork: a Jesuit, tied to a pole, being tortured by having the skin torn off his body (very graphic and violent). There was an old dark wooden clock with a swinging gong. And just the biggest, warmest arms ever, holding me, not talking, just humming her songs, comforting me, sometimes telling me stories. It was the first time I remember being happy.

That was my Grandma! Those are the memories I have of my Grandma and of her front entrance. It was an entrance into a world of absolute Love and Care for a little girl living in an unsettled world and afraid of so many things. Grandma was a "character." She had a parrot, or some sort of bird, that flew around the house and terrified my adoptive Mother in case it landed in her hair. Grandma wouldn't lock her bird up. She thought it was funny, told Mom, "Birds weren't meant to be caged," and then I remember her chuckling.

To this day I hate seeing birds in cages, just isn't right.

When I got older, there was a ceremony held in Kahnawake, where I was honoured to carry my Grandmother's traditional Name. She stayed with me as a Spirit for many years, saved my life a number of times, when I was just being stupid, or self-destructive, or lost. She often came in my dream time to talk to me, advise me. I remember seeing her in Eaton's in Toronto when I wasn't very old, maybe 12, looking at me over a counter, smiling. By the time I got to her, she'd vanished. I haven't heard from her in a while, but I feel she's smiling, pleased with me, even though

I'm not only a Mohawk anymore. But that's a whole other story, and we'll get to that later.

I had to live in libraries learning who I was, cause my Dad couldn't answer any of my questions and his relations just weren't there. Dad and I were the only non-whites around for miles until they adopted my Sister Deb...Those libraries and my love of reading gave me a base to work on when I struck out on my own to discover my People and connect. At least I had a bit of written word knowledge; then again, I carried so much more knowledge in my blood and in my dreams. The Ancestors often came to speak to me.

My nickname in school was "zombie"...Self-evident: trying to avoid school and avoid the kids when I was there, just staring straight ahead and ignoring the taunts, the shoves, till they became overwhelming... and I hit out, very violently and effectively. Or I just didn't bother going to school and found my own places to hide. To explore and learn about myself, learn about life...

Dawn with her half-sister Deb, father Walter, and adoptive mother Margaret.

NOW, HERE'S THE STORY OF HOW I BECAME AN OJIBWAY, or as I like to call myself, a Jibmok—half Ojibway, half Mohawk. I was getting older, in and out of Kahnawake, in and out of Toronto, in and out of dozens of towns and communities. Thinking at some point, I'd trip over the knowledge of my Birth Mother...We go by our mother's lineage, so it's very important. I needed to find my Siblings that were stolen from me...Got into too much drama in Toronto, between love, disappointing friendships and work, and so with a new broken heart and shattered Spirit, I changed space. I went to Alberta again...After a while, headed to the Yukon again, my land of freedom.

I was in the Yukon when I heard that the canadian government had basically declared war on the Mohawk Nation...Being a good Mohawk, off I went on the bus to stand with my People...Small problem: the night before I planned to leave, I broke my ribs in a fight I'd broken up in Dawson...held me up a few days in Whitehorse, then off I went anyhow. There were signs of support along the whole bus route...Feeling optimistic and positive, I got off the bus in Montreal, and an old French woman tried to spit on me...her spit dried up, so no problem. All right, off to the Native Women's Hostel or Native Centre or somewhere to connect... being sent in circles by everyone, till I spotted a construction worker who sent me in the right direction without a problem...knocked on the door and this cute Mohawk woman opened it and, after introductions, I told her what I needed.

She said no, she wasn't driving me to Oka; turned out she was a cousin, a Deer, according to her. She took me home with her to Kahnawake, not Oka...seems I was in the place I should be with the choppers and soldiers and crap going on...So, my Grandmother's People were here, and I found out why I hadn't been able to find them with the name I had; Grandma had changed her last name when she was living in Detroit.

I started working with social services and with Elders, checking on them. They sat, some of them, afraid in their kitchens, wondering if a soldier's bullet would come through the window and kill them, and no one would know...They had lots of fear and were just so happy to have tea and diversions from the war on our perimeter...At one point, all the Elders and Sick were to be transported off Reserve. Not all left, one old lady said she couldn't handle it if she left and they killed us all...Wise decision, thinking back.

As the Elders and Sick were leaving, there was a barrage of Montrealers aiming rocks at the cars and trucks as they drove by. One rock hit a baby in the face; another, an old man, was hit in the chest and was rushed to hospital. The police did nothing. This was a negotiated exit for the most vulnerable...no surprise at all to any of us. Another memory—a young boy went missing, very young; everyone was out looking, panicking that he'd been snatched by the military...The next day he was found. His little self, with his Mohawk Hair and his army fatigues, had spent the night sneaking up on the soldiers at the front line. Very proud of him. His Folks, though, had a very stern moment with him after! Think he was five or six.

There was all this propaganda about how heavily we were armed; we had little. There was a Brother photographed up in a tree holding what they said was a heavy military rifle; it was a fishing rod! I had a .22, some had hunting rifles, some had whatever they found handy. Like the time the military tried sneaking in where the long house was, a bunch of Our Women, armed mostly with sticks and brooms, stopped them damned quick!

The job I got was with Kahnawake Social Services, doing Family Support work, which I had a lot of experience with...Also worked out of the Literacy Centre—I'd taught literacy before and it made me very happy helping, so important...Well, there I was in this old woman's home, helping her with the housecleaning and just visiting, when she asked me who I knew in Toronto. Started throwing names out...She asked me my adoptive Father's Name and when I told her, she screamed...She kept saying my name, over and over...She was my Aunt Lillian, Father's Cousin...She knew me in the beginning, when I was first adopted...It was my Aunt Lillian who finally told me the big family secret; I was my Father's illegitimate daughter, so was my Mohawk Sister Deb. It was the times, a horrid thing to have children out of wedlock. I was in my 40's when I finally was told. So, my Adoptive Father turned out to be my Birth Father...Bizarre that he never told Me or Deb, but I can understand it now.

Now, I'll skip ahead momentarily. I rejected the welfare system that the canadian government addicted many of us to. I liked working and learning something new, never wanted the government to have control over me...Refused, when it was time to get my "status card," never wanted anything to do with the government or to be a "government Indian." Was determined to stay independent from a young age, till it was time for retirement, and I finally applied for "status."

Didn't want a canadian passport, so decided the "status card" was the lesser of the two evils. Was time to find out where I really came from and learn the story of my People. That's how I came to know that, yes, I was Mohawk, and I was also Ojibway...Half and half...Fascinating, considering all the Ojibway I hung with, and all the territory I was always drawn to.

Took years to get it. They lost my files, said I wasn't listed at Children's Aid...Told them I sent those papers in on such and such a date; they sent the wrong forms. Just too many people and too much paperwork...Every piece of paper was signed by someone else...Just normal bureaucratic nonsense, a game...Friends getting angry for me, while I was just amused, figured it was my punishment for being an activist. Anyhow, about six years later, I was finally a band member and had a status card; Indian Affairs gave me a choice, Alderville Reserve or Kahnawake or Christian Island?

I went with Alderville. Being a good Mohawk, I was now going to be a good Ojibway; we follow our mother's line and my Birth Mom was Ojibway. Kahnawake was my Dad's Reserve.

I kind of find it intriguing that Indian Affairs seemed to know he was the Father, what with him not being listed on my birth papers at all, and "father unknown" written in the records according to Children's Aid. In those times, many birth fathers' names weren't put on any government forms...How he came to adopt me, or years after, my Sister Deb, is beyond me...

—

Walking at night on the streets of a city,
cutting through a parking lot,
blackness in the middle of an array of artificial light...
feet running up behind me…a kick sends me flying,
skidding on the ground...
"fucking squaw," a kick in the head, another in the gut...
more words, more kicking feet,
colours of pain swirling...
shirt ripped open…more foul words and punches…then
silence...
a couple, two women, ask me if they should call an ambulance?
One holds a tire iron...
asks if they should call the police?
Grateful that they asked, "no point," I say,
and they fully comprehend...
They help me home, make tea, I take some aspirin...
sink down into darkness…shed some tears...
In my teens still...
very aware of what just happened...
aware it just may happen again...
seems nothing ever changes...
I get tougher...
if I'm going down,
I'll be going down fighting...
I harden up, become someone I don't want to be...
always on the lookout,
non-trusting, waiting for that first word or look...
Straight White Women learn their lessons in this world
quickly,
have some redress they can count on, if they're from the right class...
Native Women and Women of Colour and
Gay Women learn their lessons young
and quickly, there are no courts to take us seriously...

if attacked and the attacker is injured, chances are
We'll be the ones locked away...
We have no court of justice...
most Women don't report Violence or Rape...
Why should We...
How many rape kits are languishing and forgotten?
How many Native Sisters have been thrown in jail
for defending themselves or those they love?

I remember,
in a holding cell with a street sister,
a bunch of cops sniggering about which one of us
they'd like to fuck...
In a holding cell for nothing,
while they checked us out...
Both of us young...
just them trying to intimidate "the squaws,"
putting "the fear" into us,
making sure we knew "our place"…
How long is this violence against us going to be condoned?
Our Missing and Murdered Relations
across this Continent deserve an answer...
We deserve an answer...
My Beautiful,
Strong and Resilient Sisters
need to know they are safe
and respected...
All Women need to feel that...

I sat in on classes at U of T...
Hung at the courthouse or museum or library...
Went wild crafting in the park system,
Fishing in Lake Ontario,
Learning to lay snares in the bush around me...
So much to learn...
Such a barrage of violence everywhere.
Suicidal thoughts on a daily basis,
a living hell, no friends.
Not allowed to hang out with the odd boy I got along with,
just in case,
made the Mother nervous.
No girlfriends...
Wrong colour,
Not cool,
Too many reasons...

WINNIE SMOKE'S CHILDREN (the three of us, out of seven, who managed to reconnect and were reunited in our older years) all had some sort of brain impairment, or physical impairment, or both. I was very functional, but still, it was there. Impaired my memory and focus as a child, and weakened my body. In innocence and anger, I continued the same destructive path as my Birth Mother, with alcohol and drugs—mostly LSD.

I loved the experiences with acid, so nothing to apologize for there. I still think acid, music and poetry probably led me to a place where my feelings of suicide finally receded, the deep depressions finally became manageable. It helped me find the other reality: one of utter beauty and love and miraculous adventure and artistic expression. A world I could relate to and get lost in.

Probably if I had been offered professional guidance through my "trips," it would have been safer and more beneficial, but it wasn't to be. Could be, my personal control issues kept me pretty safe; I was always prepared to bring myself down, and I always had folks around me that were ready to help me, if I lost control. And my source got laboratory pure, no additives. I know others died, being out of control— some ended up in life care situations, losing themselves altogether, or burning their brains.

Just want to make it clear that what I was doing was dangerous and no one should follow what I did.

In my head I found many places in my acid dreams that were filled with truth and comfort and answers, a different and deeper plane of reality, an intenseness of beauty and colour and light. It still amazes me I'm here, that I survived...not the drugs but my forays into despair, my suicide attempts, my addictions. I survived my sometimes hard and dangerous lifestyle, from just not caring if I lived or died to a need to experience absolutely everything that I could possibly experience. The road I was led to was one of life and love and beauty and gratitude; very rocky and not without my share of PTSD, where I emote or cry with little restraint over world affairs (or someone stubbing their toe), but always in private, with no one to witness...

I REALLY DIDN'T SEE A PURPOSE FOR MY LIFE, everything just hurt so much...all the things going on in the world: atomic bombs, black people being hung from trees, little girls being bombed in Birmingham, how humans mistreated each other, how they mistreated the animals, how they dirtied everything they touched...Sure, I learned to put on a façade. No one could ever know, because it was my business what I was feeling, what I was going through.

I was strong and just didn't care what was thrown at me; I was a proud Mohawk. No one knew I was on the brink of non-existence. No one understood I was broken when a baby...and was still broken going into a bleak adult world.

We've all got our talents and I guess suicide wasn't one of mine... Too much thinking at times; standing, ready to jump off a bridge, then thinking, *what if someone sees me, or I land on a boat in the river and traumatize someone forever*? Kept my feet planted firmly...

It's good now, looking back with a sense of humour...Thank Creator and my Spirit Guides for being there for me...Life was so much more than the bleakness I was living in...I had no choice but to experience it fully; I was right into it, in the depths of depression...I would paint, and write poetry, and compose songs, and really feel it, not knowing there was an end, with colour and laughter and love and goodness waiting...

Any of you caught up in the darkness, remember me and my words: there is an end to the pain. Hang in there, keep your eyes and heart open for that first glimmer of light.

Climbing a mountain in the Okanagan with a friend, just a day climb. Small mountains, saw wild horses, a beautiful, hot day...I was on a rock face, clinging hard. A whirling goes by me. I shout her name, it takes me minutes to get off where I was clinging. There she is: scraped, a bit bloodied, stunned. A wee bush, the only one in sight, prevented her from falling over a cliff and down a mountain to her death. We continued to the top, made it down before night fall. Believe in Magic. Believe in the Spirits. You start something, finish it...No point in living with regrets.

Like many of my Peoples, particularly the traumatized, I drank. I drank heavily. I could drink any man or woman under the table; now doesn't that seem like a silly claim to fame? Whenever I got to a new town, I'd find the "Indian bar"—most towns have them.

We'd gather together at these bars to meet one another, feeling comfortable in each other's company, finding places to crash, sharing meals, being part of a community...I remember this big, ole Indian Woman coming up to my table, all tough and threatening, challenging my own perceived toughness.

Ouch, I'm thinking, but I can't lose face...We stare at each other and then she sits down and puts her arm up on the table for an arm wrestle. I smile, very slowly put my arm up, staring her eye to eye, smiling... She puts it down, without me even trying. I'm still smiling at her; she figures I'm Tough as Hell, and we became good Friends by the end of the evening. Never did tell her I faked the toughness, knew I didn't stand a chance! Well, I was tough all right, but she could have broken every bone in my body, lol...

All those "Buddies"...all of us in our 70's and 80's now. Back then, just "Young Bloods"...busy trying to have a "good time" (and slowly killing ourselves). Years later, I came to understand alcohol was provided by the colonials to help kill us off. A tool of genocide. We use it as a balm for our pain and anger; in truth it only kills Our Spirits, breaks up families, gets us thrown in jail, weakens our minds, scares Our Children and does exactly what the enemy wanted...destroy us!

I was there. Most of us were...so many of us elderly were drunks. We survived and watched our friends die. We watched as families fell apart...I remember one night, one little girl, crying and asking us to stop drinking. We did. But so many Children were allowed to fend on their own, or turn to parenting their moms or dads...

As the numbers racked up higher and higher in the jails and in the coroner's hands, many of us came to an understanding of the politics of it and how our bodies don't tolerate it...how much it has polluted and killed and destroyed Our Peoples. Understanding may help to stop this poison, I pray so. And now we worry about drugs...so self-defeating...

We don't lay judgements; we were there. We survived, so many didn't. We know the work it takes on everyone's part to end this cycle of despair. Some of the young think it's all about partying and having a good time with their friends...that's what we thought as well when young...Prayers for all.

Now I'm just surprised that
the Creator, the Universe,
has given this pitiful human so many Blessings;
granted so many Caring and Loving Humans
who surround me and enrich my life.
Grateful that through Love
I lost the violence.
Can still feel that righteous anger,
can display it with a word or look,
do not have to physically lash out.
Seems the older I get, the heart gets wiser,
the personal hurts get dulled...
the hurts that my People have suffered,
are suffering,
still bring tears to my eyes...
There is strength in those tears...
I am grateful.
Yes, racism is all part of the
canadian fabric...
We fight the way we can,

through fists,
or words,
or art,
or a rifle raised,
or poetry,
or walking,
or running,
or writing music,
or our voices singing loudly,
or dancing,
or blockades,
or theatre,
most who can fight back do,
in any manner possible...
We've had too much taken not to fight...

I think that we forget
that there are those who may not have anyone,
who are alone...
Here we are, leading full, miraculous lives every day,
while the woman next door,
or the old dude down the street,
or the teenager across the way,
struggle to fill the emptiness in their lives...
Think also there are many "solitaries"
living fulfilling, exciting lives,
but some are alone with no choice and I think
that's part of our responsibility,
sharing and caring and reaching out...
taking part in the health of the whole village.
I think that isolation is ripe ground for the beasts to come out
and display themselves.
A sense of belonging nourishes the Spirit...
not only theirs but ours as well.

WE STILL HAVE OUR YOUNG ONES, those who have fallen into a dark world where they can't see themselves ever finding hope, or love, or a future. Our suicide numbers are horrendous. Positive self-image is negligible, due in large part to racial profiling, because they constantly hear that "Indians" are useless, stupid, welfare-living, alcoholic, dirty savages, with no redeeming characteristics.

This is our world. So much control is exercised over our lives in words. This is one of the most devastating effects of racism and colonialism: the destruction of young lives, the loss of that spark in both young and old that would otherwise help them through the morass of pain.

We Anishinaabe know all about being smothered by living in a society that never really acknowledges the racism that surrounds us. If people don't acknowledge it, how could it exist? Just think about it: it does...Not only in thought and word, but also in violence and in the excruciating number of "Missing" from Our Communities, in the murdered bodies found, or lost forever. Not acknowledging this. This is "Racism." My People are easily murdered, with little or no consequence, because We don't matter to the powers that be, or to the media, or to the whole judicial system, nor to the society that is called canada, or america, or mexico. If We talk about it, or complain to the authorities, We're just "whining again," or "being overly sensitive" or "dramatic."

The figures are there; the numbers show it all. Genocide is happening and it's backed up by a society's racist attitudes, by ignorance of the facts, by the inaction of the authorities, by a society of white folks where most just don't give a damn.

We the People have to give a damn: those are Our Relations, Our Sons and Daughters and Kids who are being tortured, sexually attacked, murdered. Every single Woman killed is not just one death. That Woman represents Our Future generations. Her womb represents all of Our Future generations, the children that can never be born now, with her death. The children She may have had down the line.

These Deaths are an active and ongoing Genocide of the Original Peoples of this Land. These are the Missing and Murdered Women. And let's not forget all the Men and Children that have also gone "missing."

Those days, in the 60's and part of the 70's, it was pretty safe hitching, these days not at all. I remember line-ups on highways of kids with their thumbs out as far as you could see...was just what we did then, few problems. Flash forward, so many Native Women, Men and Kids have gone missing or been murdered...not all hitching, but for many it has become a death sentence...Flash backwards, my scariest moment was a ride I got from a cop, heading to Thunder Bay, talking about all the bodies found along that highway, and all those never found; "most were young sweet 'squaws'," he said. My hand was on my boot knife the whole way; I was never shy about pulling it or using it if needed. First pullover I saw, I said I needed to get a coffee and he pulled over to wait while I went in to get two "to go" coffees...I sat in a booth instead, just stared out at him through the window, telling the waitress about him, pointing...He drove off after that. I stayed in the restaurant till the morning came; the lovely waitress got a trucker she knew to take me the rest of the way...

There were other incidents, but this one had death written all over it... these days no one should hitch, period. Our Women, Men and Children seem to be targeted and everyone wonders why...The sexualization of Our Men and Women by media of all sorts is one reason, but I think the largest reason is our invisibility. If Our Women disappear, small notes are made, and life continues on. "Probably just got drunk and hitched somewhere else," or "decided to meet up with someone and holed up with them for a while," or "gone partying"...not taken seriously until their body is found...The numbers are increasing, not decreasing...We are invisible people in this country, and anything can happen to us, by anyone, and it means nothing.

Rape has nothing to do with Sex, but with Power, and it's guaranteed that most of these crimes are being done by white men who know they'll be safe. Rape, kill, get out of there. The rapes of those found are vicious, so we know they meant to torture and terrify before they kill. This is Hatred. This may be against Us Indigenous or against Women generally. If any energy is made to find our killers, it's an aberration when our murderer is found. Systemic racism, through society, through the police, through the court systems...

No one cares...no one but us and Creator and Our Community...and a few settlers and supporters. There's just not enough outrage from media and citizenry in general; government and police really do not care, or this wouldn't still be going on...Our grief gets deeper daily. These are not all hitching deaths; we've told everyone not to hitch, but people "walk on water" and think nothing could ever happen to them...We've said, "Don't go anywhere alone, make sure there's a backup."

Friends have gone missing together...We need the police and citizens to be working together on this and take it seriously; we need the courts to take it seriously. Check the numbers: Missing and Murdered Native Women far outnumber those of any other People...Check the numbers... We are one of the smallest populations...

To the citizens of canada: "You've got to stop the killings"...To the citizens of america: "You've got to stop killing us"...mexico even has their own Missing and Murdered as well. Altogether, the numbers in the last few years are in the thousands. Every murder represents the deaths of generations. These murders go far beyond the murder of someone's daughter or granddaughter or mother...it is generations disappearing in these sex crime murders and it is a continuation of genocide.

In Silence I release my Anger
In Pure thought I release my Pain
In Love I release my Sadness
In Forgiveness I release all Resentment

We have Our Young Ones who hold hope for us and who work
continuously towards healing our commu-
nities and the Lands and Waters.
The Young who have gone to speak at the United Nations,
who have gone and stood strong on the front lines.
Blessings to these Young People who speak from their hearts,
who seem to see the destruction happening,
while others among Our Adults see nothing.
Blessings to the Women who have taken on Leadership,
who have become Water Protectors and Warriors for Justice.
Blessings to Our Men who gave up on
the negative ways of this world,
to focus on the Protection of the Women and Children,
which is their rightful role.
Creator gave us the Responsibility of reclaim-
ing and protecting all Our Lands.
To do this, we need Everybody.
Our Families.
Our Communities.
We need to heal and give this battle the very best of us.

WHEN I WAS LITTLE, 3 or 4 years old, the Little People would come and visit me in my room at night. One time I woke up to chatter and my bed was surrounded; they were smiling and talking to me and about me, I think it was either 3 or 4 visitations...I still remember what they looked like, still remember their smiles...They were my friends. I just assumed they were real, visiting me at night, secretly. I had no idea who they were, hadn't heard the stories about them. The first time I was a bit nervous, but not afraid. After that initial visit, I was comfortable. My first memory of friendship.

Children see into other worlds, or realities; they can see the Spirits around us...As we get older we lose this ability somewhat, though I know the Spirits are still there with me...Sometimes when you need them to be, the Spirit Guides come to help out...

Sometimes you can feel them touch the top of your head, gently, a slight motion, just enough to get your attention, see if you are paying mind. There are layers upon layers of realities. Animals can see the Spirits; watch your dogs and cats...watch the deer.

I love my Memories of the Children in my life. Children have always found me. I'm an Auntie. Creator has always given us different gifts, and this was mine. I remember the Smiles and Tears and Angry Faces and Fearful demeanors from my "Kids"...now all grown and Moms and Dads and Grands to their own. I still remember the feel of a small hand in mine, walking along a dark street, just talking and looking at the stars. I remember tears from the fear of a thunderstorm and not one story I told seemed to dispel the fear a mom had inadvertently passed on...A piece of artwork that brought such a beautiful smile from a child when she could see I meant it when I said, "It is beautiful." The smile on a young one when I said how I was so proud of his accomplishment, something he'd worked so hard on.

So many memories from my Extended Family. I remember the look on a young girl's face when a Respected Elder and Medicine Woman told Her she would follow a Medicine Path when she got older...I remember the tears of a boy who told me he didn't want to go home again (booze and fighting)...Children are precious beings...we need to grow them into adults with Respect and Love and Patience. Heal the Communities. Heal Ourselves. I forget a lot, but it seems when it comes to my Kids, I remember so much.

Our Children of the Light
the Children of Prophecy
the ones we put our biggest hopes in
for the survival of Humanity
and the Land
and Waters,
for the air
and the Creatures
who walk Her,
Fly in Her,
Swim in Her,
Grow in Her...
The Waters are taking over the Lands once again.

All are one and the same to our Mother,
All equal and loved,
yet we adults need to be remembering:
Our own work here has not ended.
We still have so much work to do.
We are healing ourselves and healing these lands.
We are healing and struggling to make way for our Grandchildren.
We are here to support Our Children of Prophecy
and, perhaps, help build a better world for all.
Time is almost up, and we need to be vigilant warriors
in our roles as Protectors.

The fires in Our Mother's Heart are active and angry.
This will continue until Humanity
starts Thinking and Acting with one Mind and does right.
Give Her the medicines She needs and end the poisons.
She cannot fight off any more...
She is Sick and Sad and needs Our help desperately.
The corporations must be brought under control.
We can no longer tolerate the destruction they're causing.
Our Mother dies, All dies.

SPIRIT EXISTS IN EVERYTHING on this planet...every rock and tree and blade of grass...the waters, the air, everything...Spirits communicate between each other...communicate with us...we breathe the same breath as our Ancestors; every Baby born carries the genetics of their Mother, the DNA of the long line of those who came before them; the same rain falls on us as fell on our Great-greats...

The Plants will say, "Pick me gently and I will help heal you, human, and if picked gently, I'll also be here to heal your Great-grandchildren"... The waters will say, "That Mill is poisoning me and is on the road to killing me and all the life I hold; remember you are a part of me, human"...The trees hold each other and tell each other when death approaches and whisper to the birds and plants...

We've got to re-learn the chatterings of this planet again and begin honouring them as we should. We've worked so hard on dishonouring them that the world is dying (and not that slowly)...There is still time, but when time runs out, it will happen quickly...

TRUDEAU TALKS ABOUT "RECONCILIATION." White man's balm. White folks want to gather around and give apologies and have lovely gatherings and blanket ceremonies while my People are just trying to survive, or find a way to heal from hundreds of years of a war of extinction...

How can there be any reconciliation till all the wounds and tears they gave us are healed in my People?

"Reconciliation" puts money out there, that white folks take for putting on workshops. They talk some of us into showing up at these workshops to give themselves credibility...You know, re-reading this I sound bitter and racist; possibly I am to a degree, something I wrestle with often, because I really don't want to be a purveyor of hatred.

Our teachings don't teach hate, I really don't think it's racism I feel, but just an intense historical awareness of what has and is still happening on my continent, to my People. This government provides monies for "reconciliation" that achieves nothing for us but makes them look good on the world stage. The bruises and wounds this society has left us with at times come out in words that may hurt...I don't like hurting anyone; all colours disappear when I come to love you and that means I need to trust you, despite everything...This goes for most of my People. This society and their government need to show us that we can actually trust their words; that we can trust that the colonials, the settlers, and all others are actually trying to bring justice for my People, trying to make changes in this society.

Where are those monies that will provide clean drinking water on some of our territories that have been under water watch for years? For the clean-up of lakes and rivers polluted by the mining and resource damages done on our territories? For the proper health services needed to Heal the People after exposure to poisons leaking into our soils and waters? For the poisoning of our air? For decent housing or rectifying situations like getting 30% less to educate Our Kids?

Where are the laws and truth that ensure the corporations aren't defiling Our Waters and Lands and Air any longer? That fully protect all the habitat, keep them from logging all Our Trees, killing Our Animals and Fish? Where are the counselling programs that help us deal with our depressions, our PTSD, our lack of support systems? Our traumas from residential schools? Or the 60's scoop atrocity or the day schools? Why aren't there training facilities in green construction? Or anything dignified in the environmental area, to let us make a living with well-paying green jobs?

There are always jobs on the pipelines, in the mines, on the oil rigs—environmentally devastating jobs with no honour, where we travel miles away and leave Our Families and endanger our lives. Jobs where we help destroy Mother Earth, while Our Families are working on trying to save Her. Poisonous atmospheres, where a little more of Our Spirits die.

When will Our Children, integrated into Our own laws, with Sovereignty and dignity, will feel equal to any other child? And Our Children and young Men and Women can feel they aren't putting their lives on the line every time they leave their house...

And Our old People, Our Elders, can feel Honoured and taken care of...

ALL TREATIES MUST BE HONOURED NOW!

Our Grandfathers negotiated in good faith—but the Nations were immediately dishonoured. Honour the Treaties and all Understandings: they were negotiated as Nation to Nation. We are SOVEREIGN NATIONS. We stand aside from your Elections because canada is your nation, not ours...

There will come a day where Our People will no longer be under your control...The systems and chiefs and structures and tens of thousands of people hired to control us in your bureaucracy will be no more...It's Our Responsibility to Protect and Heal Our Lands, Our Waters and Our Peoples...Claim Your Sovereignty, My People! Break the chains of assimilated thought. We can do this with forgiveness, with no hate, but with love, because these are our teachings. Decolonize!

We can Honour Our Ancestors and still encourage Our Young to attend the Universities of the colonials. We encourage Our Young to return and work on the things we need besides knowing Our own ways and thinking and Our Histories. We need medical knowledge, we need legal training, and we need educators and accountants and historians and vets and environmental scientists and professionals of every sort.

We also need Our Young to work in the trades, milling the lumber, building our houses, putting in the wiring or septic or doing the roofing. We need Our Past just as much as We need Our Future. We need to encourage Our Kids to get an education and return and protect this Land and Our People and Our People's traditional ways as well as those who don't follow those ways...There is not one reason that you can't be a lawyer for your People and also sit in Ceremony...We are vibrant Peoples who've got so many artists and crafters and actors and musicians and designers and photographers and writers that we need to gather all these lights under one roof.

This is Sovereignty! We take what's appropriate out there and use it to Our People's benefit. This is not assimilation if we have the meat of Our Ancestry behind us. If we have the knowledge of Our ways guiding us. We are strong and vibrant Nations that are growing stronger every generation. We get nothing from being assimilated into a colonial country that derides and patronizes Us.

There is Power in the word No! Particularly when that word is spoke in Unison. We need Our Skilled, We need to Protect Our Ways, Our Traditions, Our Old Ones, everything that goes into making a Proud Nation by Governing Ourselves following the ways of Our Peoples. We have never given up Our Nationhood. Never.

Fight for Sovereignty!
Why are you voting in an alien government's election?
Learn your History,
the History of these Lands,
the History of your Peoples.
Fight for those Treaties,
Fight for Sovereignty,
not as a concept, but a reality we've never given up.
Stop buying into the lie that "you can make changes from within";
assimilating into the Power Structure of your enslavers
does not achieve a thing,
except weaken us.

You have a Nation, reclaim it!
Let's all Decolonize.
Let's all reclaim Our Nations,
Our Own Sovereignty.
Let's reclaim Ourselves.

We've reclaimed Our Own
and it's up to Us to bring Strength to Our Communities,
to end all the lateral violence,
to learn and grow and connect again
to the Earth and Universe,
to once again connect
to the beauty of ourselves and the world around us.
To reclaim everything that was taken...
to do it all through love,
not anger...
to realize we aren't victims...
Once you've taken your power back
that title dies.
We need to open our arms wide
and welcome all of us brown skins back into the circle...
Our Peoples were scattered,
we need to find them.
The Creator put us beings here for a purpose,
find what your purpose is.
Reclaim!

Decolonize...
I could go on but just want to share
that we Indigenous have so much work to do,
there is no time to sit and let others do it.
To Decolonize You need to do that Yourself
and give and lend support to others.
Learn Your Language.
Learn Your History.
Feed Yourselves.
Pick Your Medicines.
Pray and Learn the values of Your Ancestors.
Reclaim Your People, Reclaim Yourselves,
make Ceremony.
Never let anything or anyone stop You
from following where your Spirit says it
belongs...

CAPE CROKER RESERVE (now known as Neyaashiinigmiing)—I used to love going to spend time camping there.

There was a white man's camp site all fancy and mowed— trailers lined up right beside each other, clotheslines, loud music, women in curlers with too-tight clothes and men with big bellies, wearing very little...Me, I'd be on the "Indian" side, alone or with a friend, and that side was bush and a tent. Every other day I'd go up to visit the old men from the Cape Croker Reserve who hung out at the store, smoking and talking, and we became friends...

One time Old Man Johnston took me home to meet his wife; ended up staying with them...Many fond memories about that time. One of my favourites is when Old Man Johnston said he talked it over with his wife and they wanted to adopt me. In my youthful way I told them that I was honoured, but they were Ojibway and I was a Mohawk, so it just couldn't be. Years later I found out that I was half Ojibway, half Mohawk! Lol. Anyhow, loved those good folk; they taught me a lot. I hope I didn't sound as rude as my recollection, if so, I'm sure they forgave me (after a good chuckle).

One night, while camping out by the Bay, I got up to go pee and there were two oversized human eyes up in a tree, staring at me. Next day I walked up to the store and told the old men about what I'd seen. "No, not an owl...no, not any critter I've ever seen...Yes, I smudged the campsite and even laid rope."

They looked human, those eyes...That night, one of the old men joined me at my fire and then they reappeared. The old man checked it out and left without saying a word...Next day, I walked up to the store again and they told me that years long back, there was a group of Mohawk women and children, hiding out in one of the caves in the bluffs who starved to death there. The Old Men thought they showed themselves to me for a reason, and I'd know one day...

One day, yes, I found out, it was because I turned out to be part-Mohawk, and those Mohawk women's spirits had come down to visit me, maybe to protect me. We had bears and snakes in the bush there; not once did any of those critters disturb or bother me when I was out camping alone.

I loved to learn and listen; welcomed a challenge whether it was scaling bluffs or facing off a bear. Whatever the challenge, I never gave up. All I wanted to do was listen and watch and learn. The government wanted to make me into something I wasn't...I wanted to reclaim myself back.

Did a pretty damn good job— I learned how to fire a gun, or bow (pretty darn good), throw a knife, snare a rabbit, dress it down, how to fish with hook or spear, make a decent fry bread and cook for a feast, how to make some medicines and prepare for winter, how to grow my food... The learnings and teachings just kept coming and they still continue on...

Gratitude to Creator for giving me all the opportunities I've had in life to Learn. Not all of Our People have had these opportunities. I never learned my Language, because of being stolen. There wasn't much thought given to that in those days and there weren't many Mohawk Speakers around. I hung mostly with the Cree and Ojibway and few knew more than a couple of dozen words in those languages...This was the time when residential and day schools and the 60's scoop left us with little...I'm so proud of Our Young who have grasped onto the importance of Our Languages...What colonialism took from us we're reclaiming.

The only regret I have is not being able to speak much Ojibway...Many of the Stolen are older now; it's harder to learn, harder remembering... But listening to the Young speak the language sends shivers...So proud.

I remember in my dreams, or in my Spirit, things from long ago. This is Genetic Memory and I believe most of us have this. Nothing made up, but very real. The Spirits come and speak. We remember and feel things from so long ago.

Our Ancestors are with Us.
I am my Grandmother and all my
Grandmothers who came before me...
I am my Great-greats as far back as the beginning.
We are all connected.
We are Spiritually connected.
Connected in Flesh and Mind and Memory.
Every decision we make in the present includes the past
and looks towards the future.
We need to put Ourselves in the present and listen.
We've forgotten to Listen.
The voices and Memories are there.
Sit by the Waters, alone, close your eyes, be silent, listen.
Feel the Earth and Waters. Listen. Reach out.
Feel the Old ones. Hear Them.
All is a Sacred Circle.
All is Magic.

OUR MEDICINE PEOPLE ARE CHOSEN BY CREATOR...

They are not self anointed; they don't go to school to learn the ways of Spirit. It's not waking up one morning and saying, "This might be a good idea; maybe a good way to make friends, earn a living, be in the spotlight, get people to respect me" — whatever, it's not up to ourselves. It's Spirit-led. It's Creator's decision. It takes decades of learning. It may start as a dream by another, involve much contemplation and prayer, and require deciding whether or not to take someone under their wing...

The apprentice/helper serves the Medicine Person and helps and follows that Medicine Person or Spiritual Leader. The lessons learned go on till they're told it's time and much ceremony has been fulfilled... Years can go by, even decades. Many levels of achievement have to be completed; they have much difficult work to do before they even come close to being ready. They've been chosen because the Creator's spark has been seen in them during dream time, by their teacher. They've been given choices and if they've decided to devote their lives, quietly, to helping their Nation, their journey begins...The lessons and dreams are slowly shared. Being a Spiritual Leader takes so much devotion and knowledge and selflessness that few really would take the role on willingly; but then there are those who are so honoured that their demeanor takes on a glow and their Spirit walks in front of them...

No one is perfect and most would admit that...A Medicine Woman I knew told me that alcohol, ego and sex problems seem to be the weaknesses that plague the "spiritually enlightened"...seems pretty human to me...Unfortunately, some of these Medicine Men and Women cave into their weaknesses easily, so, my dear People, be cautious. This same Medicine Woman I speak of also said:

"Women should go to Women and Men to Men," she said. Women are stronger in many ways and have different roles...This also prevents any weaknesses to assert themselves from the Men; makes sense. Remember, ego is an enemy in any life and can personally defeat the strongest. Be cautious...Too many disappointments...Look and feel and ask questions... Nothing wrong with that if done respectfully. If you make a request, remember tobacco, maybe cloth and other traditional gifts are given... Remember, if you request, then proper protocol for their hard work and the honour of their time and gifts needs to be respected. These times, along with cloth and tobacco and medicine herbs, remember that food helps, and money is needed for household expenses.

Back in the old times, we took care of Our Elders, everything from shelter to food. Our Medicine People were taken very good care of, because they took very good care of us. Before the time when paper money became a god, life was so much easier and practical. Now many need to pay for phones and mortgages or cars; keep that in mind when asking for help. We tend to expect Our People to serve us for nothing, that's not the way it works. You ask for something, then you honour them for the gift they attempt to give you. We, all of us, take care of them. They shouldn't have to ask. They are honouring you, by carrying these gifts and sharing them. Be respectful. If you know any Elder is suffering in any way, then make sure the need is taken care of. Simple. Again, on genetic memory, I figure we all possess this connection to the Old Ones...Don't know how to do something? Sit back, give it some thought or focus and ask direction from them...The answer is there inside you...Do this and listen when the Elders speak, don't be asking them your hundreds of questions...Over time, maybe a lifetime, your answers to your questions will all become evident. Honour those who carry gifts, including yourself.

Don't take everyone who calls themselves a "Medicine Man" (or "Medicine Woman," or "Spiritual Leader," or "Healer") at Face Value. Even some Pipe Holders are led by their ego, some aren't even Anishinaabe. Some are fakers and have been corrupted by "greed" and "ego;" love their ego strokes, feeling special and making money...Ask around...

In the Old Way, you find the trusted ones; they are quiet, they are humble. They don't need ego stroking or idolization, they don't advertise, put on weekends that cost hundreds of dollars, have an inordinate number of non-Natives taking part in ceremony (or following them around). They don't dress up and pretend they walk in wisdom, when they don't live that way. They don't drive the nice cars, wear the nice clothes...Find the humble and quiet ones, bring your tobacco and cloth and ask for what's needed. Go to your own People; if you're Cree, or Ojibway, or Blackfoot, or Sioux, or whatever Nation, go to your own...Men go to men; women go to women...We all have our own ways...

Things are becoming homogenised between the Nations; some things are o.k., but we need to be holding on to what has always been the core of our own nations. That is a step towards claiming our own Sovereignty; claiming our own ancestral power and honouring our own Nation, learning to speak our own Language, learning our own Histories, honouring ourselves and our Ancestors.

We are all one Nation among many Native Nations among many other Nations on Mother Earth, the Great Turtle. We gather in Circles to pray and celebrate; some prefer to do it silently and alone. No one owns the truth. The only thing important is what You Do, period. Not Judgements about skirts, or silent prayers, or where the berries are placed. A "church" dictates how things are done. Our Spirituality is natural and needs no dictating. How much heat was in the sweat lodge and how you handled it is ego. How you can pray in "the language" when so many can't (for reasons perhaps of genocidal policies) is ego. Comparing your relationship with Creator as "special" is ego. No one is above anyone else and only Creator chooses who to listen to...Be proud of what you do know and willingly share; just don't allow "ego" to trip up your feet, or tongue, or spirit.

Jealousy, envy: these are not, nor ever were, Our ways...Speaking bad, holding grudges, judging others, greed...cast these things away... They don't belong to any of Our Peoples. Remember the Grandfather Teachings...remember the Grandmothers'...Bring no shame on Your Peoples...Help all Heal.

Our relationship with Creator is not a "church."
Our relationship is one of silence
and song
and meditation
and love.
It can be communal or singular...
It is not, and never was, meant to be a "church."

Our Birth
is only a continuation of Life.
Our crossing over
is only a continuation of Life.
Life is a never-ending circle
Nothing actually dies
Just takes on a new form
Spirit or Solid
It continues on.
All is a Circle.

You are Stardust,
You are Blessed,
The Spirits Smile because You are here.
You are here in all your humble beauty,
an Indigenous Child,
an Indigenous Woman,
an Indigenous Man...
and You are Love and Strength and Beauty.
Always Remember
The Ancestors are walking with You,
all you need to do is recognize Them.
Welcome Them in.
Open Yourself up to Possibilities.
Open Yourself up to the Universe.
Creator Is with Us all.
Feel and Live,
Breathe and Give,
See and Listen and Acknowledge.
Gratitude always.
Do what You Do with an Open Heart
Expect no Thanks
No ego strokes
Just accept that Creator knows Everything
Be Humble.

Walk Softly
Speak Softly
And Keep your eyes open.

SO, THERE WE GO, I did remember some things, gave you stuff to ponder on, hopefully, reminded you maybe of your own memories—like a sunset that was so beautiful it made you cry. Or the smell of a flower that mesmerised you.

The one thing about memory I noticed, when I was recalling, is that I also had smell and colour to go with those memories, and those particular senses I can't share. The texture of a moment is just as important as the recall. I mentioned my PTSD...well, when I was adopted, I also was suffering from something called "Reactive Attachment Disorder." I put my adoptive parents through a lot, but then if I wasn't stolen from my mother to begin with by the 60's scoop mentality, all would have been fine in that area perhaps. It wasn't the adoptive parents' fault, but it also wasn't mine...

There have been so many People in my life, and I've done so many things and travelled so many roads that there are thousands of memories, and my mental "filing system" just gets overwhelmed. I'm grateful for each and every one of those People who have shared a bit of my life, both negative and positive, and have appreciated the "colour" they have added to my canvas.

From a kid who felt alone, unloved and angry, I proceeded to grow into a Strong Anishinaabe Kwe, whose main passions are the Earth and Her Living Entities and of course Her Wonderful Brown People, and all the amazing Friends of every Gender and Hue that share my life. This includes especially all my wonderful extended Family members; some I've had for 50 years, some are Daughters, some are Sons, some are Nieces, some are Sisters or Brothers and Nephews, a whole whack of Cousins… some are very close and well-beloved Friends.

I have a Fount of Love and gather some very special Souls into my Circle. What I've shared here is no big thing, just one story of millions. I've learned so much on my journey here this time around and feel very Blessed right now, being given the opportunity to share some of it. Yes, I've been very Blessed.

I encourage all you Elders out there to write your stories down; there lies some of Our History. There was a time when your story would be kept in hearts and memories and be shared on Winter nights. Your Grandchildren and Family would take courage from your story, and they would still be learning the lessons you'd learned, perhaps generations from now. These days Our world is larger, and Our Stories are easily lost. It's important that your story continues on, all our stories; this is Our Legacy for Our Youth, Our lives, Our gift to the future. Our respect for the past, written in the present…

Thank You for allowing me to Share.

Miigwetch.

Dawn Smoke, November 11, 2019

About the Author

Dawn Smoke is the daughter of an Anishinaabe mother (Ojibway) and Mohawk father. She has been an artist, sculptor, creator of jewelry, and occasional poet for some 50 years. A Survivor of the sixties scoop, Dawn was moved between foster homes until she was adopted at three years old. She has worked in and for the Native Community for most of her life. She was the co-founder of the Native Women's Resource Center in Toronto and she has served on many Native boards and in Native organizations, including the Toronto Warrior Society and Idle No More projects. Dawn is grateful to have spent her life traveling across many territories on Turtle Island. More recently, she has returned to her home territory in Alderville, where she lives in seniors housing. There, Dawn feels renewed by her Ancestors' strength.

About the Illustrator

Jacqueline "Jackie" Traverse was born in Winnipeg, Manitoba. She is Ojibway from the Lake St. Martin First Nation. Jackie began drawing as a child and was inspired from a field trip to the Wahsa Gallery when she was 13 years old. It wasn't until she was 32 years old that she decided to submit a portfolio of her works to the University of Manitoba where she studied Fine Arts and graduated with a diploma in May of 2009. Jackie Traverse is widely known in art communities across Canada. Her paintings, drawings, documentaries, and sculptures speak to the realities of being an Indigenous woman. To Jackie, painting is truly where her heart lies.